Prayer Works
for Teens
Book 1

Prayer Works for Teens Book 1

Lisa-Marie Calderone-Stewart

Saint Mary's Press
Christian Brothers Publications
Winona, Minnesota

Genuine recycled paper with 10% post-consumer waste.
Printed with soy-based ink.

The publishing team included Robert P. Stamschror, development editor; Rebecca Fairbank, manuscript editor; Holly Storkel, typesetter; Rick Korab, Punch Design, cover designer; Maurine R. Twait, art director; pre-press, printing, and binding by the graphics division of Saint Mary's Press.

The inside illustrations are by David Chang and Lisa-Marie Calderone-Stewart.

The acknowledgments continue on page 68.

Printed in the United States of America

Printing: 9 8 7 6 5 4 3 2 1

Year: 2005 04 03 02 01 00 99 98 97

ISBN 0-88489-432-0

Contents

This book is dedicated to
David L. Chang
1958–1994
David, you gifted me with imagination and spirit.
You stretched my religious boundaries
to help me form new images for faith and worship.
You taught me to see all of life as art and service,
and to see all of prayer as exploration and discovery.

Author's Acknowledgments

Thank you, Ralph, for exploring prayer (and life!) with me in so many creative ways. And thank you for resurrecting an entire chapter from the secret caves of computer storage when I unintentionally deleted twelve hours of work with the push of a single button.

Thank you, Mom, for the joy you share in my ongoing work. The best part of being an author is having such a delightfully proud mother!

Thank you, Bishop Lawrence McNamara, for appreciating my work, for supporting me during all my writing projects, and for giving me the opportunity to serve the youth and adults in the Diocese of Grand Island.

Thank you, Lilleth Chang, for keeping in close touch with me since David's death, and for going through all of David's artwork, in search of whatever might fit the needs of *Prayer Works*. Your son was amazing. So many of us miss him deeply and look to that glorious day when we will see him again.

Thank you, Bob Stamschror, for your critical eye and your challenge toward excellence. Knowing you has made me a better writer and a better person.

Thank you, Bishop Ken Untener, for being a major influence on my spiritual formation, my ministry, and my life.

Introduction
to *Prayer Works*

Prayer works. It really does. Or does it?

Does it work for you? When you try to put together a meeting or an event, what's the hardest part to plan? the icebreakers and games? the theme presentations? the small-group discussions? the large-group activities? or the prayer time?

If you're like many youth ministers, the prayer time is the most difficult to plan. Why? Is it because prayer really *doesn't* work, or because it's really challenging to find ways to pray that are suitable and meaningful for teenagers?

You probably wouldn't be involved in ministry if you truly thought that prayer doesn't work. So, more than likely you just need some help finding ways to pray with young people that connect with who they are and what's important in their lives.

Perhaps you also need a renewed sense of what to expect from teenagers. For instance, if you use the same worship experience with a peer ministry team of high school seniors at a leadership training retreat, and then with a group of seventh graders at an all-night movie lock-in, can you expect the same degree of involvement and prayerfulness? Probably not.

Sets of Prayer Experiences

Here's what *Prayer Works* offers. Each of the four books includes three sets of prayer experiences. Each set consists of four prayer formats: a short prayer, a medium-length reflection prayer, a long ritual prayer, and a family prayer. Every prayer set focuses on a different image or object. The three focus objects in this book are a rock, an aloe plant, and children of God.

To find out what the focus objects are for the other books of *Prayer Works*, check the back cover of this book. And while you're checking, note what comes at the end of this book. You'll find that the prayers for all four books are indexed by Scripture citations and themes.

The prayer experiences in each book are easy to lead, but you will need adult volunteers to help you with many of them.

Short Prayer

The short prayer can stand by itself, or it can be the introductory prayer at an event that will include an additional prayer or two with the same focus. The short prayer is perfect for that situation when you want to start off with some sort of prayer, *but* . . . —*"but* everyone doesn't know one another yet," *"but* teenagers will be feeling awkward and it probably won't be too prayerful," *"but* it can kill your event to get too involved too soon with anything deep or complex." You probably know what I mean.

So this first prayer is short and sweet. It reminds us of our connection to God, quiets down the participants, focuses them, and gets them ready to begin. *But* it isn't so long or cumbersome that the young people start getting restless.

Medium Prayer

The medium-length prayer can stand by itself, or it can be the second prayer in a series of two or three prayers that you lead at an event or class. It is a faith-sharing prayer that involves self-reflection using Scripture passages or comments, reflection questions, and a conversation with a partner or small group. This prayer has an accompanying handout that contains the Scripture passage(s) or comments and the reflection questions. Directions for using the reflection part of the medium prayer follow. The directions are customized to apply to three different types of groups.

Self-Reflection and Sharing with a Small Group

If you have a group of fewer than fifteen teenagers who know one another well, give everyone a copy of the reflection handout, found at the end of the prayer set. Direct them to listen while the Scriptures and comments are being read, and then to jot down some thoughts or feelings that are triggered by the reflection questions. Naturally, you will always have some folks who aren't "jotters" or journalers, and there is no need to pressure them to write if they don't want to. But giving the participants time to reflect quietly, whether it is in their head or on paper, is very helpful if faith sharing is expected in the group.

One effective way to use this reflection method is to have volunteers read the different sections of the handout. For example, if the handout is arranged in this order—Scripture passage, comments, and questions—then one person reads the Scripture passage, a second person reads the comments, and a third person reads the questions, pausing after each question so that everyone (including the readers) can reflect and jot down their thoughts. That pattern would be repeated for the next set(s) of Scripture passage(s), comments, and questions.

Using different voices for different sections of the handout will help everyone listen more carefully. It's easier to listen when different people alternate reading, as long as every reader speaks with a clear, confident voice that can be heard and understood.

Allow everyone to share verbally with the group. This can be done in a random, spontaneous, whoever-is-ready-to-share-can-share method. Or it can be done with an ordered, go-around-in-a-circle-and-share method.

Often the focusing object (for example, a rock) can be used as a turn designator for this type of prayer. When it's time for sharing, you, as the prayer leader, pick up the object first, offer your reflections, and then pass the object to the next person to do the same. Or, after you pick up the object and offer a reflection, you place it back in the center of the group and whoever else is ready to share can pick up the object and start sharing.

By the way, not only does the focusing object make an excellent turn designator, it also does a fine job of helping people forget that everyone is watching them. It can be awkward for some people—especially teenagers, but adults as well—to talk to a group when everyone is looking at them. Having an object to fiddle with can distract them from that awkward feeling and help them feel more comfortable.

The prayer experience can be ended with the closing reflection included in the prayer set or with any spontaneous words you think are appropriate.

Self-Reflection and Sharing with a Large Group

If you have a group larger than fifteen and don't want to separate the young people into smaller groups for the process just described, you can change the dynamics of this experience by not distributing the reflection handout to everyone. Instead, tell everyone to find a partner to share with. Call on designated readers to read the Scripture passage(s), comments, and questions from the handout. As each question is read, the partners can share with each other. You might direct the young people to switch partners periodically if you are trying to build community in your group. Or you might direct them to keep the same partner if you are more concerned with developing fewer but deeper relationships. End the prayer experience with the closing reflection or words of your own choosing.

Self-Reflection and Sharing with a Journaling Group

If you intend to have the group write in a journal, have the Scripture passage(s), comments, and questions from the handout already written on a chalkboard, piece of poster board, or overhead projector. Everyone can then write the questions in their journal, respond to one or more of them, and then join a journaling partner for a faith-sharing walk. Because this type of sharing disperses the group, it doesn't always work well to end the activity with a closing reflection, but that's up to you as you plan your event and assess your group's needs. Sometimes you might want to regather and close as a unified group; other times you might want to let the partners' sharing flow into a break or meal and have no official closing.

Long Prayer

The long prayer can stand by itself or serve as one in a series of two or three prayers at an event or class. This prayer involves more creativity and ritual than the short and medium ones. It is difficult to describe or summarize because it varies so much from prayer set to prayer set. The long prayer, as its name suggests, usually takes the most time, but it depends on your group and the situation. Here are examples of the processes in some of the long prayers in the four books of *Prayer Works:*

◆ In book 1, the long prayer with the rock image focuses on the strength and permanence of virtues and principles. It involves painting words on actual rocks.
◆ In book 2, the long prayer with the nuts image focuses on the importance of God in a life of many choices. It involves creating a faith carrier out of a jar of rice and walnuts.
◆ In book 3, the long prayer with the four seasons image focuses on the seasons and repeating patterns in our life. It involves a prayer journey to four different environments.
◆ In book 4, the long prayer with the puzzle image focuses on the puzzle of sin and on finding our peace (as well as our piece) in a reconciliation service. It involves working with puzzle pieces.

Family Component

The most unique aspect of *Prayer Works* is the family component. So often families have no idea what their teenage members do at parish events and retreats. But *Prayer Works* gives you an easy way to involve parents and siblings in the prayer experienced by the teen. Two items make up the family component: a family handout and a sample letter for families.

Family Handout

Each set of prayers includes a handout containing a family faith-sharing prayer. The family handout is modeled after the medium prayer handout, but the teenager does *not* need to have experienced that prayer for the family handout to be effective. The family handout includes directions and questions designed for use in family settings. You can photocopy the handout and use it in one of the following settings:

A gathering of families after a retreat or long event. End a youth retreat or other event with a family meal. Invite all the parents, brothers, sisters, and whoever else may share your young people's homes with them. After the meal, invite several young people to get up and share about parts of their prayer experience by telling stories, doing skits, or showing examples of what happened.

The families can then share their answers to the questions on the handout. Even young children can participate in answering most of the questions. In this way, the families not only have some idea of the kind of experience their teenagers had but also share in the experience itself.

A separate gathering of youth and families. Hold a reunion for the teens who participated in an event or retreat, and invite all their family members to attend. Or just have a gathering for the young people you work with and their families. In either case, after a meal, do an activity that involves storytelling or skits related to the event in which the prayer was used, or just distribute the family handout and move the family groups into conversation using the faith questions.

A bulletin or parish newsletter insert. Use the family handout as a bulletin or parish newsletter insert. This is a wonderful way to spread the good news about what young people in your faith community are doing. Write a brief article about the event in which you used the related prayer forms with the young people. Include other folksy details about where you were, the history of the event, or some of the related activities. Explain that you are providing this family prayer handout as a service to *all* families, whether or not they had a teenager who attended the event, and that you hope it helps spread the kind of spirit the parish's young people experienced at the event.

A personal letter and take-home handout. Send a personal letter home to the parents of the participants, highlighting parts of your group's event or retreat, and thanking them for making the family arrangements that were necessary for their teenager to attend the event. A sample letter for families (described below) is included at the end of each set of prayers for you to use as a guide in composing your own letter.

A follow-up mailing. A few days after the meeting or event, mail the family handout to the parents of the young people who attended, along with a letter of explanation.

Sample Letter for Families

At the end of each set of prayers, a sample letter for families is offered for possible use with the family prayer handout. Be sure to customize the letter to match the prayer and the setting in which it was used. And be sure to personalize the letter by using the names of the young people and parents. If you do not have access to a computer to make this feasible, then you could ask a few volunteers to type up the letters for you. Simply supply the basic text, with a list of the names and addresses of the young people and their parents. You'll find this extra effort goes a long way.

Benefits of the Family Component

If you are hesitant about including a family component in your plans, please consider the benefits. If you get to know your young people's families, the young people will be more apt to come to future events because their parents will feel a greater attachment to you and your parish. The parents will be more likely to call on you in an emergency because they have developed trust in you, and they will also be more likely to say yes when you need volunteers. Besides, taking care of family needs and helping families develop their faith is a wonderful way to improve the lives of your young people. So how can you go wrong? That's a winning combination!

Prayer Works for Youth Leaders, Parents, and Peer Ministers

Don't worry about how to pull off these prayers—each one is simple to do and has already proven successful with teenagers. And the instructions are very specific and easy to follow, which makes it possible for peer ministers, parents, and youth leaders to run the experiences. For instance, material that is to be presented aloud to the group is highlighted with a black rule at the left margin. Teen leaders who are looking for prayers to facilitate will like these because they get the participants involved. Moreover, the prayers in each set have the same format, and that makes it easy to add icebreakers or related activities with a similar focus.

If the teens can do it, so can you. All you need is a little faith. So relax. Remember, prayer works. It really does.

Prayer Set 1
Rock

Short Prayer

Themes
- ✦ the strength of rocks and their sacredness to the Lakota people
- ✦ faith that is solid as a rock

Background Information

Although this prayer is short, its theme is broad. It brings together the symbols of rock as strength and solidity, as a metaphor for faith, and as a sacred object to the Lakota people.

The Lakotas are a Native American people with a rich prayer heritage. The rock prayer is only one of their many traditions. When you speak of the Lakota people, it is important that you always show respect so that the participants in your prayer experience see the rock and its significance to the Lakotas prayerfully and reverently, never comically or disrespectfully.

Preparation

Supplies
- ☐ a rock

Setting

This prayer can take place almost anywhere, with the participants arranged in almost any position. They can sit around a meeting table, on the floor, or on couches and chairs spread out around the room. They can even stand. Because the prayer is so brief, it doesn't require a distraction-free environment. As long as the participants can hear the words and see the speaker, the prayer can be effective.

Expectations

This prayer works equally well with junior high youth, senior high youth, and adults. It is short, to the point, and informative, and sets the mood to go forward into your meeting, event, retreat, class, or other gathering.

Procedure

If you want to emphasize the rock to the participants, hold it in your hand. If you have a very large and heavy rock, put it in the middle of the area where the participants are gathered.

The prayer is simple. Proclaim the words in a clear and confident voice. If you have an active and restless group, you might first ask them to quiet themselves so that they can become more aware of the presence of God.

Prayer | Rock—*inyan*—is the oldest thing that can be found on earth. It is sacred to the Lakota people. Rocks are so important to them that it is often said that the Lakotas "worship rocks." Of course they do not worship the rocks themselves, but they use the rocks as a way of getting in touch with the Great Spirit, God. The Lakotas often go to special large stones to pray. They can think of nothing more ancient than the rocks. The rocks have been around before anything or anyone else. No one can remember a time or history that existed before the rocks did. The message and meaning of the rocks are only for those who know how to be open and listen. (Based on Zeilinger, "The Rock," *Sacred Ground,* pp. 68–70)

The Scriptures tell us that because Simon said he believed Jesus to be the Messiah, the Son of the living God, Jesus called him Peter, "the rock." Jesus told Peter that on this rock foundation the church would be built.

Rocks are solid. Rocks are dependable. Rocks are strong. We all want to be "solid as a rock." We want to own "a piece of the rock." Folksingers have a song that proclaims, "Jesus is the rock that rolls my blues away."

Let us pray that during our time together our faith will become as solid as a rock. Let us pray that we will develop a Christian bond that has the strength of a rock. Let our prayer echo the prayer of David in the Hebrew Scriptures, who sings, "Life to Yahweh! Blessed be my rock! Exalted be the God of my salvation!" (2 Sam. 22:47 or Ps. 18:46, NJB). Amen.

Medium Prayer

Theme ◆ life events that give us strength

Background Information

This prayer focuses on rock as a solid, strong result of several processes—processes that people also go through as they become stronger and more "solid" human beings.

The prayer gives the participants a chance to reflect on how rock is formed and how they, as persons, are formed. It is a bit of a science lesson as well as a self-reflection.

Preparation

Supplies
☐ rock(s)
☐ a candle, cross, or other object(s) symbolic of Christian worship
☐ copies of handout 1–A, "A Meditation on Rocks"

Setting How you arrange the prayer participants depends on the size of your group. Very small groups can sit around a table, in a circle on the floor, or in chairs. Larger groups can spread out around the room. Set up one central focusing area in the middle of a table, the middle of the room, or along a wall that everyone can see. Place in the focusing area a large rock or a number of rocks, and a candle, standing cross, or other object(s) symbolic of Christian worship. Lead the prayer in or near the focusing area.

Expectations This prayer works well with junior high and senior high youth. Just expect that the sharing offered by older youth will be deeper than that coming from younger youth. And in either case, a group of people who know one another well will feel more comfortable than a group of strangers.

Procedure

Opening Reflection Explain to the group that with the help of rocks as focusing images, they will spend some time thinking about their lives and how certain events have helped to make them who they are. Then proclaim the opening Scripture reading found on handout 1–A, "A Meditation on Rocks," or ask a volunteer who is an excellent reader to do so.

Self-Reflection and Sharing Use handout 1–A for self-reflection and sharing. This part of the prayer can be done with small groups, large groups, or journaling groups. Details for using the handout with each of these types of groups are included in this manual's introduction, on pages 8–10.

Closing Reflection If a meal is to follow the self-reflection and sharing, you could announce ahead of time that the meal will begin right after the self-reflection and sharing and thus the group will not have a formal gathered closing.

If you are going to have a closing reflection, the prayer in this section is offered as an option. You can either read it yourself or ask a volunteer who is a good reader to do so.

You could instead end the self-reflection and sharing with words of your own, or ask the small groups or prayer partners to end their time together with spontaneous prayer. Use whatever seems most fitting for your group, your setting, and your time schedule.

> "The Rock"
>
> The rock lays near
> While light comes and goes
> The rock only exists
> Said to have no soul
> The rock cannot be sad
> It knows not the time
> It has no life to hold
> It can't feel love
> As we admire it
> It remains in stillness
> Yet in its own way
> May watch!
>
> (Lloyd Carl Owl, a Cherokee,
in American Indian Prayers and Poetry, n.p.)

Long Prayer

Theme ◆ recognizing virtues in ourselves and others

Background Information

This long prayer focuses on virtues as the mark of a holy life and the rock upon which our faith community is built. It has a Lakota influence. The Lakotas are a Native American people whose traditions have a deep spirituality. Be sure to model reverence for the Lakotas and their customs so that the group approaches the prayer with respect.

The prayer includes a craft project. The participants are asked to reflect with their prayer partner, choose a virtue that captures their partner's personality, and paint that word (along with any decorations they want to add) on a rock.

Also included in this prayer are an affirmation of the participants and a blessing.

Preparation

Supplies
- ❑ a fist-sized rock for each participant, plus some extra
- ❑ a table, crate, wheelbarrow, tarp, plastic tablecloth, or colorful bedsheet
- ❑ slips of paper, with each participant's name written on a separate slip
- ❑ eight copies of handout 1–B, "Virtue Readings"
- ❑ a paintbrush for everyone, plus extras (Try out the paintbrushes ahead of time to be sure they aren't too thin or too thick to work well.)
- ❑ cups of water for cleaning paintbrushes
- ❑ water-based paints in bright colors (Ask the folks at your local craft store which kind of water-based paint they recommend for rocks. You'll want one that won't wash off easily once it has dried.)
- ❑ posters or a chalkboard list of all the virtues mentioned in the readings: purity, knowledge, patience, kindness, truth, faith, hope, love, compassion, humility, gentleness, tolerance, forgiveness, joy, peace, goodness, faithfulness, self-control, generosity, courage, respect, wisdom, bravery, patience, dignity, and ability to provide for others
- ❑ a cassette or CD of soft instrumental music and a cassette or CD player

Setting

Set up two spaces—a prayer space and a work space. The prayer space needs to be an open area so that everyone can sit in a circle, perhaps on the floor (if there is a rug or carpet squares) or in chairs. This prayer experience will not work very well in a church that has stationary pews.

In the center of the prayer space, set up a wheelbarrow, crate, or table to hold all the rocks. Or, if your group will be sitting on the floor, place the rocks on a tarp, plastic tablecloth, or colorful bedsheet to avoid obstructing the participants' view of one another. Because the participants will be using the rocks, be sure to have more rocks than people. That way even the last person can have a choice of rocks, and the remaining rocks will serve as focusing objects.

Rocks the size of your fist are good—they are big enough to write a word on, but not so heavy that they are a burden to carry. If necessary, wash the rocks before the prayer experience. Be sure there is plenty of time for them to dry before the prayer service. You might want to ask each participant ahead of time to bring a rock, and then have a few extra on hand. But that strategy can be risky, because many of the participants may forget to bring a rock.

The work space needs to be large enough for all the participants to spread out and have room to paint on their rock. Have containers of paint spread out across worktables, with two or three brushes by each one. Each brush can have a masking tape "flag" that indicates the color of paint it goes with. Labeled brushes will encourage the participants to move to a different brush when they want to switch colors, thus keeping the paint colors from mixing.

Write the list of virtues on poster board or a chalkboard. Use large enough print to ensure that the list can be read from across the room.

Expectations Mature high school youth who know one another well will have no trouble with this prayer. You can expect them to be prayerful and reverent. Some will deeply ponder which virtue to choose for their partner, and they will want to give clear examples of when they have observed their prayer partner demonstrating that virtue. Some will even continue to see the prayer rocks as holy objects. Others might express a further interest in Native American spirituality. Please encourage that if you can!

Younger high school youth who have been together before will also do quite well with this prayer. But if they don't know one another too well, they might feel a little self-conscious about putting their hands on the shoulders of their prayer partner, which this prayer asks them to do. They also might not want to shout out the words at the end of the prayer. Just let them participate to the degree that they feel comfortable.

Junior high youth will do fine with the readings if they are read loudly and clearly. You can expect the young people to want to fool around with the paints, so I suggest you have several adults walking around the worktable(s) to discourage behaviors such as flinging paint or wiping paint on one another.

Junior high youth will also probably giggle a little when they have to put their hands on the shoulders of their prayer partner at the end of the prayer, but there's nothing wrong with their expressing their feelings of awkwardness with an innocent giggle. Again, the key is to have adults sitting with and among the youth.

Junior high young people will no doubt have difficulty trying to explain why they chose a particular virtue for their prayer partner, so don't let the explanation time lag too long. They might not have a lot to say and could begin to feel self-conscious. In fact, they probably won't even know what all the virtues mean, so be ready if they start asking for some definitions!

Overall, this is a good prayer experience for junior high youth because of the freedom of movement during most of it. They probably won't mind shouting at the end of the experience. When it's over, they might remember that rocks are important to Native Americans, and perhaps they'll also remember that somebody actually thought they had a virtue, and they have a rock to prove it!

Procedure

Call to Prayer   1. Establish partners for the rock painting by putting the slips of paper with the participants' names on them in a container, pulling them out two by two, and reading them aloud. Make sure that you, as the leader, also have a prayer partner. Then say something like the following to bring everyone together in the spirit of prayer:

> I invite you to enter into the spirit of the Lakota sacredness of prayer rocks. Please come forward, choose a prayer rock, and sit beside your prayer partner.

2. Have the participants come forward, choose a rock, and return to their place. Continue setting the mood for the prayer. Use these words, or similar words of your own, to bring out the importance of virtues and their connection to the Lakota people, who go to rocks to pray:

> People of God have always known that living by holy virtues and good values is the secret to a holy life. Saint Paul knew it, and the Lakota people know it as well.
>
> I invite you to hold on to your prayer rock as we listen to the word of God, as written by Saint Paul to the Corinthians, the Colossians, and the Galatians, and as passed on by the tradition of the Lakota people. We will even hear some words in the Lakota language.

Prayer Readings   Distribute handout 1–B, "Virtue Readings," to eight people who are excellent readers, whose voices can be clearly heard and understood by everyone. Assign one of the readings on the handout to each person. Go over the Lakota words with them so that they can pronounce the words with confidence. Give the following introduction and then direct the readers to share the readings with the group:

> Think of your prayer partner as you hear these holy words, and try to recognize which of these virtues you have observed in your prayer partner.

Response to the Prayer Readings   Move everyone into the work space with these words or similar ones of your own choosing:

> I invite you to think about what primary virtue you have observed in your prayer partner. You will have the opportunity to paint the name of that virtue on your prayer rock as a gift for your partner. We have prepared for you an area with paints, paintbrushes, and cups of water. A list of all the virtues has been posted as a reminder. After everyone has finished painting their prayer rock, we will return to this space to present our prayer partner with our gift. Please feel free to move toward the work area as soon as you feel ready.

Along with paints, paintbrushes, and cups of water, the work area also needs to include the list you prepared of every virtue mentioned in the readings. Play soft instrumental music in the background so that the young people are not intimidated by silence in the room.

When all the participants have finished painting their chosen virtue on a rock, gather the group in the prayer space, using words similar to these:

> At this time, I invite you to come back to our prayer space and to sit down with your prayer partner and explain why you chose that particular virtue for her or him. Then give your partner the prayer rock as a gift.

If you are concerned about paint getting all over the place, have the participants leave their rock on the table to dry instead of bringing it back to the prayer space. Just direct everyone to tell their partner what virtue was chosen for them. The participants can pick up their rocks later when the paint is dry.

Sending Forth   As you lead this part of the prayer, stand beside your own prayer partner and together model the body posture, gestures, and words for the group. Use these or similar words:

> I invite you to stand and enter into the spirit of David, who praised God after God delivered him from all his enemies, especially Saul. Please lift up your arms toward heaven and repeat each phrase after me so that we can praise God together:
>
> I love you, Yahweh, my strength. [Participants repeat.]
> You are my rock and my salvation. [Participants repeat.]
> I take my shelter in you, because you will protect me.
>   [Participants repeat.]
> For this I will praise you. [Participants repeat.]
> I will try to be a rock of strength for your church.
>   [Participants repeat.]
>
> (Adapted from Ps. 18:1–2,49)
>
> Now I ask you to face your prayer partner. The oldest person in each pair should speak first. First speaker, put your hands on your prayer partner's shoulders. Look into your partner's eyes and say his or her name aloud. [They say the names.]
>
> Now say these words to your partner: "You are a rock for our church." [Participants repeat.]
>
> All right, now say aloud the word you painted on the prayer rock for your partner. [They each say their word.] Then say these words to your partner: "That is the virtue I have observed in you. [They repeat.] On the rock foundation of your virtue, [They repeat.] our faith and our church is being built." [They repeat.]

All right, now I ask you to switch roles. Second speaker, put your hands on your prayer partner's shoulders. Look into your partner's eyes and say her or his name aloud. [They say the names.]

[Repeat the blessing prayers used for the first partner. Then continue.]

All right, now everyone can face one another in a circle. Put your hands into the air, and let's say some of David's words together again. Let's shout them out! Just repeat each line after me:

Life to Yahweh!
Blessed be my rock!
Exalted be the God of my salvation.
Amen.

(Ps. 18:46 and 2 Sam. 22:47, NJB)

Family Component

Details for using the family component are included on pages 11–12 of the introduction to this book. Here are a list of the supplies you will need and a reminder of the settings in which the family component can be used.

Supplies
- ☐ handout 1–C, "Family Meditation on Rocks"
- ☐ sample 1–A, "Sample Letter for Families"

Settings
- ◆ a gathering of families after a retreat or long event
- ◆ a separate gathering of youth and families
- ◆ a bulletin or parish newsletter insert
- ◆ a personal letter and take-home handout
- ◆ a follow-up mailing

A Meditation on Rocks

Opening Scripture Reading

Life to Yahweh! Blessed be my rock!
Exalted be the God of my salvation.

(2 Samuel 22:47, NJB)

Opening Comments

Rocks are strong, solid, and dependable. We want our faith to be strong, solid, and dependable. We want our relationships to be strong, solid, and dependable. We even want our self to be strong, solid, and dependable. How do we develop those characteristics? The same way rocks do.

Reflections and Questions

Igneous Rock

Igneous rock is formed from hot magma within the earth. As the magma surfaces, it becomes lava. When it cools, it hardens into igneous rock.

A volcanic eruption is a major event. Whenever a volcano erupts, it is reported in newspapers and live footage appears on TV news shows.

Questions
Sometimes we acquire strength through major life events.
✦ What major life event has given you strength? What happened? How did it affect you?
✦ What can you learn about yourself as you look back on that event?

Handout 1-A: Permission to reproduce this handout for use in your program is granted.

23

Sedimentary Rock

Sedimentary rock is formed by sediments, or small bits of matter deposited by water, ice, or wind. The sediments can be shell particles, animal bones, plant remains, or bits of other rocks. These get cemented together and hardened into layers. Sedimentary rock is the result.

These parts of plants, animals, shells, or other rocks can be very tiny, insignificant pieces of matter. By themselves, they are nothing remarkable. But put together, they form something strong and solid.

Questions

Sometimes we acquire strength from a lot of little "nothings," such as family traditions, things our parents always tell us, what our friends do, the ways we tend to see things.

✦ What insignificant little nothings have actually given you great strength? How have these little events affected you?

✦ What can you learn about yourself as you look back on those happenings?

Metamorphic Rock

Metamorphic rock is formed when already existing rock is changed by great heat, pressure, or some chemical action. Metamorphic rock is created by transition. It already is rock, but then it becomes a different kind of rock.

Questions

Sometimes we acquire strength through a transition in our life. Adapting to change brings us growth, flexibility, and a new outlook on reality.

✦ When has a change in your life given you strength? What happened? How did it affect you?

✦ What can you learn about yourself as you look back on that change?

Closing Prayer

"The Rock"

The rock lays near
While light comes and goes
The rock only exists
Said to have no soul
The rock cannot be sad
It knows not the time
It has no life to hold
It can't feel love
As we admire it
It remains in stillness
Yet in its own way
May watch!

(Lloyd Carl Owl, a Cherokee, in *American Indian Prayers and Poetry,*
edited by J. Ed Sharpe [Marietta, GA: Cherokee Publications, 1985], no page)

Virtue Readings

Reader 1. By our purity, knowledge, patience, and kindness we have shown ourselves to be God's servants—by the Holy Spirit, by our true love, by our message of truth, and by the power of God. (2 Corinthians 6:6–7, TEV)

Reader 2. Generosity. *Wa-can-tog-na-ka.* . . . A person is looked up to not only for their ability to provide food, clothing and shelter, but also for the ability to give generously and not count the cost. It is better to give a lot than to have a lot and keep it for yourself. (Ron Zeilinger, *Sacred Ground: Reflections on Lakota Spirituality and the Gospel* [Chamberlain, SD: Tipi Press, 1986], pages 56, 60)

Reader 3. Meanwhile these three remain: faith, hope, and love; and the greatest of these is love. (1 Corinthians 13:13, TEV)

Reader 4. Courage. *Woo-hit-ik-a.* Taking care of others means that a person needs to have bravery or courage. It means having to face hard and difficult things for the sake of others. . . . [People] learn to face danger without running away, and how to face even death with dignity. (Zeilinger, *Sacred Ground,* page 61)

Reader 5. You must clothe yourselves with compassion, kindness, humility, gentleness, and patience. Be tolerant with one another and forgive one another. (Colossians 3:12–13, TEV)

Reader 6. Respect. *Wo-wac-in-tan-ka.* In order for people to live together in peace, they have to respect one another. The old are respected for their wisdom and the young because they are the future of the people. This attitude also means a reverence for all other living things in the world. . . . All people and things are relatives. . . . The outcome of this respect is peace in families, among tribes and other people. (Zeilinger, *Sacred Ground,* page 61)

Reader 7. The Spirit produces love, joy, peace, patience, kindness, goodness, faithfulness, humility, and self-control. (Galatians 5:22–23, TEV)

Reader 8. Wisdom. *Wok-sa-pe.* The knowledge and wisdom of the old people is very important for the well-being of the people. They know how to give "good advice" to others because they have seen many things happen and change. . . . Wisdom is knowing that a person is nothing without the power of God. Being humble and caring for others is the wisest power of all. (Zeilinger, *Sacred Ground,* pages 61–62)

Family Meditation on Rocks

As a family, you could sit down and go over this meditation together. One family member might read the opening Scripture passage, and then others could take turns reading the comments and questions. Then you could share your answers to the questions, along with any other insights you may have.

A family member might read the closing prayer to conclude the sharing. Keeping a rock on or near your kitchen table would reinforce your commitment to keep your family's faith as strong and solid as a rock.

Opening Scripture Reading

Life to Yahweh! Blessed be my rock!
Exalted be the God of my salvation.

(2 Samuel 22:47, NJB)

Opening Comments

Rocks are strong, solid, and dependable. We want our faith to be strong, solid, and dependable. We want our family relationships to be strong, solid, and dependable. We even want our self to be strong, solid, and dependable. How do we develop those characteristics? The same way rocks do.

Reflections and Questions

Igneous Rock

Igneous rock is formed from hot magma within the earth. As the magma surfaces, it becomes lava. When it cools, it hardens into igneous rock.

A volcanic eruption is a major event. Whenever a volcano erupts, it is reported in newspapers and live footage appears on TV news shows.

Questions
Sometimes we acquire strength through major life events.
✦ What major life event has given our family strength? What happened? How did it affect us as a family and as individuals?
✦ What can we learn about ourselves as we look back on that chapter of our family life?

Sedimentary Rock

Sedimentary rock is formed by sediments, or small bits of matter deposited by water, ice, or wind. The sediments can be shell particles, animal bones, plant remains, or bits of other rocks. These get cemented together and hardened into layers. Sedimentary rock is the result.

These parts of plants, animals, shells, or other rocks can be very tiny, insignificant pieces of matter. By themselves, they are nothing remarkable. But put together, they form something strong and solid.

Questions

Sometimes we acquire strength from a lot of little "nothings," such as family traditions, things our parents always tell us, what our friends do, the ways we tend to see things.
✦ What insignificant little nothings have actually given us great strength? How have these little events and practices affected us as a family and as individuals?
✦ What can we learn about ourselves as we look back on those small chapters of our family life?

Metamorphic Rock

Metamorphic rock is formed when already existing rock is changed by great heat, pressure, or some chemical action. Metamorphic rock is created by transition. It already is rock, but then it becomes a different kind of rock.

Questions

Sometimes we acquire strength through a transition in our life. Adapting to change brings us growth, flexibility, and a new outlook on reality.
✦ When has a change in our family life given us strength? What happened? How did it affect us as a family and as individuals?
✦ What can we learn about ourselves as we look back on that change in our family life?

Closing Prayer

"The Rock"
The rock lays near
While light comes and goes
The rock only exists
Said to have no soul
The rock cannot be sad
It knows not the time
It has no life to hold
It can't feel love
As we admire it
It remains in stillness
Yet in its own way
May watch!

(Lloyd Carl Owl, a Cherokee, in *American Indian Prayers and Poetry*, edited by J. Ed Sharpe [Marietta, GA: Cherokee Publications, 1985], no page)

Sample Letter for Families

Dear _____,

It has been a pleasure having _____ with us. Thank you for making all the necessary family arrangements so that <u>she/he</u> could be with us. It was truly a gift from your family to our parish community.

During our time together, we focused on the symbol of the rock. In fact, _____ may have been given a rock to bring home. If so, a virtue has been painted on the rock—a virtue that was seen in _____'s personality. Perhaps you might ask _____ to see the rock. Praising certain virtues is a Lakota tradition as well as a Christian tradition. Saint Paul lists Christian virtues in many of his letters in the Christian Testament.

We spent some time listening to passages from those letters and thinking about virtues that reflect who we are. We also discussed the sacredness of prayer rocks in the Lakota tradition. You might ask _____ to share memories from the experience.

We also did a reflection prayer based on the types of rock that are formed from the forces of nature. Enclosed is a copy of a family-based version of that reflection prayer. I encourage you to take some time during or after a family meal to go through the questions and discuss them as a family. You could even give a small prayer rock to each person as part of the discussion, or leave a rock on your kitchen table for a while to remind your family that you want your family relationships to stay as solid as a rock. These are just a few ideas to help you get in touch with _____'s experience with this prayer.

If you have any questions about our programs, or if any of your family members would like to become more involved with our parish in any way, please don't hesitate to call me. I wish your family great peace and joy.

Sincerely,

_____

Prayer Set 2
Aloe Plant

Short Prayer

Themes
- healing
- connection to God

Background Information

This short prayer focuses on themes symbolized by the aloe plant. The prayer reminds us to stay connected with God, as the leaves are connected to a plant. Without God, we will wither and dry up like leaves that have fallen off the plant. The prayer also speaks of the healing powers of the aloe plant, which is another way the aloe plant symbolizes God.

Preparation

Supplies

❑ an aloe plant (You need an aloe plant for the medium and long prayers included in this prayer set. If you are only going to use this short prayer, then it is possible to eliminate the first paragraph of the prayer—the only part that refers to an aloe plant specifically—and substitute another plant for the aloe.)

Setting

This prayer can take place almost anywhere, with the participants arranged in almost any position. They can sit around a meeting table, on the floor, or on couches and chairs spread out around the room. They can even stand. Because the prayer is so brief, it doesn't require a distraction-free environment. As long as the participants can hear the words and see the speaker, the prayer can be effective.

Expectations

This prayer works equally well with junior high youth, senior high youth, and adults. It is short and uses three concrete examples that relate to the aloe plant. Because very little abstract thought is involved, you can expect everyone to be able to pay attention and stay interested during the reading of this short prayer.

Procedure

Proclaim the words of the prayer in a clear and confident voice. If you have an active and restless group, you might first ask the participants to quiet themselves so that they can become more aware of the presence of God.

Prayer 1. First, describe the aloe plant in words similar to these:

> The aloe plant is often called the burn plant or the healing plant because of the healing properties of its juices. For that reason, a lot of people keep an aloe plant in their kitchen. If they burn themselves cooking, they break off a piece of the aloe plant and rub its juices into their skin. [Demonstrate this by breaking off a piece of the aloe plant and squeezing out some its juices onto your hand.] The aloe helps their skin heal.

2. Next, introduce and read a passage from the Scriptures:

> In the Gospel of John, Jesus tells us:
>
> "I am the vine;
>   you are the branches.
> Those who live in me and I in them
>   will bear abundant fruit,
>   for apart from me you can do nothing.
> Those who don't live in me
>   are like withered, rejected branches."
>
> (John 15:5–6, INT)

3. Continue by introducing and reading a Krishna parable:

> A very similar parable is told by a swami of the Krishna Consciousness. The Krishna movement is rooted in Eastern meditation. The swami has written this:
>
> By pouring water on the root of the tree, all the parts of the tree are automatically nourished. Only those branches and leaves which are detached cannot be so satisfied. Detached branches and leaves dry up gradually despite all watering attempts. Similarly, human society, when it is detached from the Personality of Godhead like detached branches and leaves, is not capable of being watered, and one attempting to do so is simply wasting energy and resources. (Swami Prabhupada, *Srimad Bhagavatam,* canto 1, p. 62)

4. Conclude with the following reflection:

> If we are not connected to God, then nothing beneficial is really going to reach us. Our deepest and fullest life comes from God. So without God, all the joys of life aren't quite enough. All the miracles of modern technology can't feed us. Even the most sophisticated irrigation equipment cannot bring water to a leaf that is detached from the root of the plant. We must be connected if we want that life-giving water. That's what heals us. That's what nourishes us. That's what gives us life.
>
> So now we pray that our time together will be a time of healing, nourishment, and new life. May we be connected to God like leaves are connected to the vine, and may we be watered with the life of the Spirit. We pray that our efforts today bear abundant fruit, and we ask all this in the name of Jesus. Amen.

Medium Prayer

Themes
◆ growth and health
◆ pain and healing

Background Information
This prayer focuses on human growth and healing, using the analogy of a plant's growth and healing.

Preparation

Supplies
☐ an aloe plant
☐ a candle, cross, or other object(s) symbolic of Christian worship
☐ a copy of handout 2–A, "Lessons from the Aloe Plant," for each participant

Setting
How you arrange the prayer participants depends on the size of your group. Small groups can sit around a table with the aloe plant in the middle, or in a circle on the floor with the plant on a cloth in the center of the circle. For larger groups, chairs can be arranged in a circle, with the plant on a table so that it can easily be seen. Add to the focusing area a large candle, cross, or other object(s) symbolic of Christian worship. Sit or stand near the plant to lead the prayer.

Expectations
This prayer works equally well with junior high and senior high youth because it asks concrete questions and gives concrete examples. Mature and highly motivated young people will likely give more expanded answers and will engage in deeper sharing.

Procedure

Opening Scripture Reading
Welcome your group to prayer. Distribute handout 2–A, "Lessons from the Aloe Plant." Tell the participants that they will be learning lessons from the plant world, especially from the aloe plant, and that they will be able to see how people have a lot in common with plants, because both plants and people need to be healthy in order to grow and thrive.

Call the participants' attention to the Scripture reading on the top of their handout. You can either read it yourself, have another excellent reader read it to the group, or ask all the prayer participants to read it aloud together.

Self-Reflection and Sharing

Use handout 2–A for self-reflection and sharing. This part of the prayer can be done with small groups, large groups, or journaling groups. Details for using the handout with each of these types of groups are included in this manual's introduction, on pages 8–10.

Closing Reflection

If a meal is to follow the self-reflection and sharing, you could announce ahead of time that the meal will begin right after the self-reflection and sharing and thus the group will not have a formal gathered closing.

If you are going to have a closing reflection, the prayer in this section is offered as an option. You can either read it yourself or ask a volunteer who is a good reader to do so.

You could instead end the self-reflection and sharing with words of your own, or ask the small groups or prayer partners to end their time together with spontaneous prayer. Use whatever seems most fitting for your group, your setting, and your time schedule.

"The Cathedral of the Serengeti"

The acacia
The umbrella acacia
The cathedral of the Serengeti

This shaded chapel
    is our place to stop
        to rest
        to listen
        to be shaded
        to be comforted
        to be nursed
        to be healed
        to be still
        to be.

The walls of acacia shade like
    the walls of our cathedral like
    the limits of our baby planet like
    the covers of our Bibles like
    the bodily covers of our lives are
        windows of the Infinite Invisible.

There,
under your acacia
be frisky like weldebeest calves,
    before a rain
    with a breeze on your nose,
    with a gleam in your eye,
    with your heels higher than your ears.

I'm sure God sits there, delighted
    under the Serengeti acacia.

(Fr. Don Larmore)

Long Prayer

Themes
- ♦ the paschal mystery, death, and resurrection
- ♦ sacredness and blessing
- ♦ healing and unity

Background Information

This long prayer focuses on the aloe plant as a symbol of healing. A very large and well-developed aloe plant is needed. No other plant will do. During the prayer, the aloe plant is removed from its pot and put on the floor or ground. Dirt gets everywhere, and it almost seems as if the plant has been killed. But the large aloe plant is actually a collection of many smaller plants that continue to grow larger and give birth to new shoots.

Everyone will take a shoot of the aloe plant to repot in their own vessel of soil. Be sure that your aloe plant is large enough to have enough shoots for every person in your group. A large, full plant should have forty or more shoots. If in doubt, keep an extra aloe plant handy. But chances are you won't need it!

This prayer gets a little messy when the aloe plant is taken out of its pot. It can be done outside on the grass or inside on a white cloth. (The cloth will look somewhat like a shroud.)

The prayer will run more smoothly if people are chosen ahead of time to do the following tasks:

- ♦ Assist with the potting soil (two or three people—more if your group is very large—each with a bag of potting soil, to hold the bag open to help those scooping soil out of the bag fill their vessels).
- ♦ Remove the large aloe plant from its pot (two people to hold the plant shoots and pull up, a third person to hold the pot and pull down in order to separate the plant from the pot). These same people will be called on to repot whatever pieces of the aloe plant are left.
- ♦ Water the new plants (two or three people with watering cans, more if your group is very large, to go among the participants and water their new plants).
- ♦ Read the opening reading and the individual planting ritual prayers (two people to do all the prayers, or a different pair to do each prayer).

When the prayer is over, the cloth with the excess dirt can be taken outside (if you aren't already outside) and shaken in an appropriate area.

You need to choose the kind of vessel your group will use for potting. You can use earthenware planters if your group is not too large and you don't mind spending the money. Or you can use something less expensive, such as polystyrene cups or the bottoms of milk cartons covered with paper. The main advantage of the earthenware planters is a bit of elegance. The main advantage of the polystyrene cups or milk cartons, besides the low cost, is that your group can decorate them ahead of time, for example, during an activity period if you are using this prayer as part of a retreat or an extended day program. Eventually, small holes will need to be poked through the bottoms of the cups or milk cartons in order for the water to drain properly.

Preparation

Supplies

❑ a large aloe plant
❑ *optional:* the lyrics to "Earthen Vessels," by John Foley *(Glory and Praise,* vol. 1 [Phoenix: North American Liturgy Resources, 1977], p. 17), if your group likes to sing
❑ a vessel for each prayer participant: earthenware planters, polystyrene cups, or milk carton bottoms
❑ a copy of the readings and prayers for each part of the planting ritual (pp. 36–39), one for each person who will be reading
❑ potting soil, enough to fill all the individual vessels
❑ a scoop for each bag of potting soil
❑ a white drop cloth
❑ watering cans filled with water, enough cans to water all the individual plant vessels

Setting

Your setting needs to be large enough for everyone to sit or stand in one circle. If the weather is good, you might gather outside. If inside, find a place with a tile or vinyl floor because the dirt will probably make a mess, even with a drop cloth beneath it.

Expectations

This prayer works equally well with junior high youth, senior high youth, and adults. Expect older, more mature participants to have a deeper experience of the paschal mystery as reflected in the healing power of the aloe plant. Expect younger, less mature participants to have a neat experience of relating to God through plants.

This prayer works especially well with a group of graduating seniors and their parents. The obvious symbolism of newer plants separating from the parent plant can unearth feelings and thoughts that are hard to communicate otherwise.

Procedure

Call to Prayer

Invite everyone to gather in a circle around the aloe plant. If your group is musically inclined and enjoys singing, open with the song "Earthen Vessels," by John Foley. If your group is not musically inclined, or doesn't enjoy singing, welcome the participants to the prayer with words similar to these:

> I invite you to bring forth your earthen vessels and gather to praise our rich and fertile God, who gives us the succulent aloe plant and blesses us with one another.

Reading

Arrange for an excellent reader to proclaim these words:

> It was Yahweh, our God, who said, "Let light shine out of the darkness."
>
> It is the Spirit of God who shines from our hearts and enlightens us with the glory of the Risen Christ.
>
> This glory, this immense power, is God's divine power, not our own power. It is a treasure that we hold in ourselves, in earthen vessels.
>
> How can light come out of darkness? How can a plant grow out of dirt? How can life come out of death? It may seem foolish, but it is God's way.
>
> Yahweh chooses fools to shame the wise, and the weak to shame the strong. True wisdom and true strength are God's divine power.
>
> By the Spirit of God, this divine power exists in us also. It exists in our divine souls held within our human bodies— it's our holy treasure held in earthen vessels. (Adapted from 1 Cor. 1:27–30 and 2 Cor. 4:6–7)

The Planting Ritual

Earthen Vessel Prayer

Have everyone bring forward their vessel. Arrange the participants in a circle so that they can see one another. Ask them to hold their empty vessel in front of them as this earthen vessel prayer is read:

> **Part 1**
> These earthen vessels will hold a treasure of life—
> a living, breathing creation of God that will continue to grow as long as we choose to nurture it. These earthen vessels will give our plants space and protection to grow safely.
>
> **Part 2**
> Blessed are the homes in which we live—homes that give us space and protection to grow safely. And blessed are our bodies, the earthen vessels that hold our souls, the temples of the Holy Spirit.

Earth Prayer

Invite the people who will help distribute the potting soil to bring their bags and scoops to different areas of the circle, creating three or four distribution sites. Direct the participants to slowly approach one of the sites to receive a scoop of potting soil for their vessel, and then to return to their spot in the circle. Ask them to hold their vessel full of soil in front of them as this earth prayer is read:

Part 1

This soil will embrace the roots of our plants. Our plants will nestle deeply into it, and the nutrients and minerals of the soil will nourish our plants so that they can grow stronger.

Part 2

Blessed are the earthy people in our lives. Blessed are the nurturers who have embraced us and held us. Blessed are the people we love and feel comfortable around—those who allow us to nestle deeply into their soul so that we can grow stronger. And blessed are we when our lives are entwined with the nurturing of others.

Plants and Growth Prayer

Invite the people who will remove the aloe plant from its pot to come forward. Direct the person pulling the pot down to kneel, and the others supporting the plant and pulling it upward to stand. It won't take long for their gentle action to separate the plant from the pot. Direct the person holding the pot to take it to the outside of the circle, while the others gently lower the aloe plant, now in pieces, to the ground or the white cloth on the floor. Once the helpers have returned to their places, have everyone face the plant as this plants and growth prayer is read:

Part 1

This one plant has been growing for years. It was a large, full, strong plant. It will be divided up into many smaller plants. It will be broken apart, separated, transplanted, and scattered, so that its healing can become a part of all our lives.

Part 2

Blessed are the people in our world who give their lives to serve others. Blessed are we when we remember the needs of the forgotten and when we make choices to bring fuller life to others.

Healing and Unity Prayer

Invite everyone to use one of their fingers to dig a hole in the soil in their vessel, and then to come forward, pick up one of the aloe plant shoots, and plant it in their vessel. After the participants have planted their shoot, have them return to their place in the circle. Direct the people who removed the plant from its pot to return and repot the pieces of it that are left over. Once everyone is finished, have them stand in the circle, holding their plant in front of them as this healing and unity prayer is read:

Part 1

These tiny plants will begin a new life with each of us. Uprooted and scattered, they need time to adjust, time to be nurtured, time to grow stronger. If cared for, each of them will become a large, full, healthy plant, separate from its parent plant but still united by its nature and essence. Its soothing juices will be a healing presence to us.

Part 2

Blessed are the people of our world who are uprooted and scattered, in search of unity and belonging, in need of time for healing. Blessed are we when our brokenness brings forth unity and healing.

Water Prayer

Invite the people who will water the plants to come forward with their watering can. Direct them to stand near the center of the circle, facing outward at the others who, also in a circle, are facing inward at them. Have the waterers hold their watering can in front of them as this water prayer is read:

Part 1

This water, which at one time fell from the heavens to the earth, will quench the thirst of our plants. It will moisten and seep into our plants and become part of the plants' own life juices.

Part 2

Blessed are the people who are our lifelines. Blessed are the people who quench our thirst for truth and sprinkle our lives with the waters of holiness. Blessed are we when we work for justice and empower others to keep growing.

Gardeners' Prayer

Direct everyone holding a plant to remain in their place while the waterers come around and water the plants. Be sure the main aloe plant in the middle is watered as well. Once the watering is done, have the waterers place their watering can on the ground or the floor near the main aloe plant and return to their place in the circle. Once all are standing at their place in the circle, invite them to hold their plant in front of them as this gardeners' prayer is read:

Part 1

These plants are entrusted to the hands of these gardeners. These gardeners will nurture their plants and see that the plants are provided with God's sunshine and water, and with new soil and new space when their roots have outgrown the limits of their earthen vessel.

Part 2

Blessed are the gardeners in our lives who care for us, provide for us, and give us space when we have outgrown our previous limits. And blessed are we as we come to appreciate the struggle of balancing needs.

Closing Reflection

For a closing reflection, you have several options. You could invite the group to sit down and share their feelings and thoughts about the planting ritual. This sharing could take place in pairs if you have a large group, or all together if the group is small enough to give everyone a chance to be heard in a short amount of time.

Or you could offer your own reflections about the group and its life together. If this is a retreat group, a leadership training group, or a graduating class, a special message relevant to those events could be given.

If you have a meal planned to follow this prayer, you could end with an invitation to join the meal, and the meal's blessing would be the closing of this prayer.

You could end by singing "Earthen Vessels" again, if your group likes to sing.

You could end this prayer with spontaneous words of your own choosing, or a simple blessing with the sign of the cross.

Family Component

Details for using the family component are included on pages 11–12 of the introduction to this book. Here are a list of the supplies you will need and a reminder of the settings in which the family component can be used.

Supplies

☐ handout 2–B, "Family Lessons from the Aloe Plant"
☐ sample 2–A, "Sample Letter for Families"

Settings

◆ a gathering of families after a retreat or long event
◆ a separate gathering of youth and families
◆ a bulletin or parish newsletter insert
◆ a personal letter and take-home handout
◆ a follow-up mailing

Lessons from the Aloe Plant

Scripture Reading

"Along both banks of the river, fruit trees of every kind shall grow; their leaves shall not fade, nor their fruit fail. Every month they shall bear fresh fruit, for they shall be watered by the flow from the sanctuary. Their fruit shall serve for food, and their leaves for medicine." (Ezekiel 47:12, NAB)

Lessons and Questions

Lesson 1

Growth can be physical. As plants grow, they become crowded and need more space. Similarly, we grow out of our clothes as we become bigger.

Growth can also be psychological. We can grow out of the decor of our bedroom, or out of old habits or restrictions that are too childish for who we are now. We can even grow out of a friendship if we have grown and our friend has not.

Questions

◆ When has your growth caused you to feel cramped and uncomfortable?

◆ What adjustments have been necessary to accommodate your growth?

Handout 2-A: Permission to reproduce this handout for use in your program is granted.

Lesson 2

When a plant has completely outgrown its space, it needs to be transplanted. This can cause some shock to the plant's system, and it takes awhile for the plant to adjust.

Some moves we make are because of our own growth—into a new bedroom or into the next grade in school. Some moves we make are because of our parents' growth, such as a job promotion that takes us to a new city or a new state.

Questions
✦ When have you had to move? How did it feel to be "transplanted"?
✦ Did it "shock your system"? If so, how did you adjust? If not, why not?

Lesson 3

For us to be healed by the aloe plant, we have to break off a piece of it. The plant heals with its own life juices, but then that part of the plant is wounded, and it takes time for it to grow back again and to heal itself.

When we are hurt, it takes time for us to feel better again. Caring about others sometimes takes a lot out of us.

Questions
✦ Where are you "broken"? When have you been hurt? Did time heal your wounds? If so, how?
✦ Have you ever been able to help someone else who was hurting, even though you too were hurting?

Lesson 4

A healthy plant needs consistent sunshine, water, and nutrient-rich soil. A gardener cannot put off caring for plants for weeks at a time and then try to cram in all the water, light, and plant food at the last minute. That would not yield a healthy plant.

It takes time and discipline to care for a plant, and it takes time and discipline to do the things we need to do for school, work, friends, and family.

Questions
✦ Which of your needs and chores do you take care of in a healthy way?
✦ In what situations do you procrastinate and then try to "cram" at the last minute?

Family Lessons from the Aloe Plant

As a family, you could sit down and go over this family meditation together. One family member might read each lesson, and another might read each set of questions. Then you could share your answers to the questions, along with any other insights you may have.

Scripture Reading

"Along both banks of the river, fruit trees of every kind shall grow; their leaves shall not fade, nor their fruit fail. Every month they shall bear fresh fruit, for they shall be watered by the flow from the sanctuary. Their fruit shall serve for food, and their leaves for medicine." (Ezekiel 47:12, NAB)

Lessons and Questions

Lesson 1

Growth can be physical. As plants grow, they become crowded and need more space. Similarly, we grow out of our clothes as we become bigger.

Growth can also be psychological. We can grow out of the decor of our bedroom, or out of old habits or restrictions that are too childish for who we are now. We can even grow out of a friendship if we have grown and our friend has not.

Questions
✦ What have the children in our family grown out of? When has growth or change caused uncomfortable family stress?
✦ What adjustments have been necessary to accommodate such growth and change?

Handout 2-B: Permission to reproduce this handout for use in your program is granted.

Lesson 2

When a plant has completely outgrown its space, it needs to be transplanted. This can cause some shock to the plant's system, and it takes awhile for the plant to adjust.

Some moves we make are because of the children's growth—into a new bedroom or into the next grade in school. Some moves we make are because of the parents' growth, such as a job promotion that takes us to a new city or a new state.

Questions

✦ Has our family ever had to move? If so, how did it feel to be "transplanted"? How did our family adjust? What was the hardest part? What was the best part?

✦ If our family has never moved, we may have experienced transplantation on a trip. What was it like when our whole family or only some members of our family spent one or more nights away from home? Who traveled? Who stayed home? What was the easiest and most difficult part of the trip to adjust to?

Lesson 3

For us to be healed by the aloe plant, we have to break off a piece of it. The plant heals with its own life juices, but then that part of the plant is wounded, and it takes time for it to grow back again and to heal itself.

When we are hurt, it takes time for us to feel better again. Caring about others sometimes takes a lot out of us.

Questions

✦ When has our family suffered some pain? Did time heal the family wounds? If so, how?

✦ When did we as a family cause ourselves pain? Have we been able to help one another with our hurting? If so, how?

Lesson 4

A healthy plant needs consistent sunshine, water, and nutrient-rich soil. A gardener cannot put off caring for plants for weeks at a time and then try to cram in all the water, light, and plant food at the last minute. That would not yield a healthy plant.

It takes time and discipline to care for a plant, and it takes time and discipline to do the things we need to do for school, work, friends, and family.

Questions

✦ Which of our needs and chores do we take care of in a healthy way? In what situations do we procrastinate and then try to "cram" at the last minute?

✦ What's the effect on the family when everyone is trying to cram and take care of their own needs at the same time? How can we reduce this kind of stress in the future?

Sample Letter for Families

Dear _____,

It has been a pleasure having _____ with us. Thank you for making all the necessary family arrangements so that she/he could be with us. It was truly a gift from your family to our parish community.

During our time together, we focused on the aloe plant. The aloe is often called the burn plant or the healing plant because of the healing properties of its juices. If you burn yourself, you can break off a piece of the plant and rub its juices into your burned skin. It will soothe the pain of a first-degree burn (pinkish skin with no blisters and no breakage of skin).

Enclosed is a family-based version of a reflection prayer we used with our group. I encourage you to take some time during or after a family meal to go through the questions and discuss them as a family. _____ was given a small aloe plant to take home and care for. You might ask about it. Keeping the plant on the kitchen counter or table for a while might serve as a reminder of your family commitment to be healers for one another. These are just a few ideas to help you get in touch with _____'s experience with this prayer.

If you have any questions about our programs, or if any of your family members would like to become more involved with our parish in any way, please don't hesitate to call me. I wish your family great peace and joy.

Sincerely,

_____

Prayer Set 3

Children of God

Short Prayer

Themes

+ humility
+ the "kindom" of God

Background Information

This short prayer reminds us that becoming like humble children is the way to get to heaven, and it speaks of heaven in terms of the "kindom" instead of the more traditional "kingdom."

Kingdom implies a place ruled by power, with subjects and royalty, with haves and have-nots. Kindom evokes imagery of people who care about one another because they are family or close enough to feel like family—a place where everyone's needs are met and people watch out for one another.

Preparation

Supplies

☐ a few children's toys, perhaps three or four building blocks or a top (If you also intend to do the long prayer with this group, consider using a paper chain—with only three paper links or so, in bright primary colors like red, yellow, and blue—instead of the other toys. That will make the connection between this short prayer and the long prayer obvious.)

Setting

This prayer can take place almost anywhere, with the participants arranged in almost any position. They can sit around a meeting table, on the floor, or on couches and chairs spread out around the room. They can even stand. Because the prayer is so brief, it doesn't require a distraction-free environment. As long as the participants can hear the words and see the speaker, the prayer can be effective.

Expectations

Both adults and senior high youth react positively to this prayer. A junior high group may be less willing to think about childhood because they are still close to their own childhood and are struggling to remove the label "child" from themselves. However, if the members of a junior high group are highly motivated, they are likely to respond positively as well.

Procedure

Proclaim the words of the prayer in a clear and confident voice. If you have an active and restless group, you might first ask the participants to quiet themselves so that they can become more aware of the presence of God.

Prayer

1. Begin with words similar to these:

> The Gospels tell us about a time when Jesus' disciples asked him about greatness: Who's the greatest? Who's the best? Who's number 1? Jesus didn't tell the disciples it was the king or the pharoah. Jesus didn't say it was the pope or the prime minister, or the group with the song at the top of the charts, or the team who won the championship game. Number 1 is not the actress from the most popular TV show and not the president of a billion-dollar corporation.

2. Then read what Jesus said in the Scriptures:

> "The truth is, unless you change and become like little children, you will not enter the kindom [We are talking *kindom* here, not *kingdom*.] of heaven. Those who make themselves as humble as this child are the greatest in the kindom of heaven." (Matt. 18:3–4, INT)

3. Continue with the following reflections:

> So first *we* have to change. In other words, if we are asking whether we are the greatest in the kingdoms of the world, then we're not even asking the right question!
>
> Second, we need to be like children or else we don't even have a shot at making it into the kindom.
>
> Third, if and when we do make it into the kindom, the ones who are greatest are the ones who are most humble.
>
> So during our time together, let's try not to be concerned about the wrong things. Let's not try to be the greatest in terms of power, control, and popularity. Let's ask the right questions. Instead of asking, How can I be the best in the room? let's ask, How can I best serve the others in this room?
>
> Let's try to make this place a kindom: a place where we all feel like kin, a place where it's natural for us to take care of one another, a place where we can all feel like children—safe, open, curious, and able to see the goodness in everyone.

4. Conclude with the following prayer:

> Almighty God, who takes delight in the little ones,
> help us to be your children.
> Bless us with humility,
> and teach us to be servants for one another.
> Show us your vision of kindom,
> and keep us close to you.
> We gather in your name today
> to continue to do your work and bring you glory.
> Amen.

Medium Prayer

Themes

✦ children of God
✦ the status of a child
✦ relationships between "old" people and "young" people

Background Information

This prayer focuses on what it means to be a child and what a child's status is. The Scripture passages used, from both the Hebrew Scriptures and the Christian Testament, are practical as well as imaginative.

Preparation

Supplies

☐ a paper chain or child's toy
☐ a cross, candle, or other object(s) symbolic of Christian worship
☐ copies of handout 3–A, "Children of God"

Setting

How you arrange the prayer participants depends on the size of your group. Small groups can sit around a table, in a circle on the floor, or in chairs. Larger groups can sit in chairs arranged in a big circle. It works best to have one central focusing area in the middle of the table or in the center of the circle. Place in the focusing area a paper chain or child's toy and a large candle, cross, or other object(s) symbolic of Christian worship.

If you are planning to use the long prayer with this group as well, it might be best to use a paper chain as the focusing object.

Expectations

As with the short prayer, this medium-length prayer may not work well with a large group of junior high youth if they are not motivated to participate. If you do use the prayer with junior high youth, focus on the questions that are easiest for them to answer.

Procedure

Opening Reflection

Tell the group that they will spend some time focusing on what it means to be a child of God. Explain that children are typically free and imaginative. They have a sense of wonder that is sometimes lost when they get older. Mention that the participants are going to hear a short African prayer for spontaneity and for that wonder of childhood. Have an excellent reader proclaim the following reflection:

Great God, be filled with song and joy;
receive the songs of all people.
You who live on high.
You alone who lead us.
You who created us.
You who protect us.
All that we have is yours.
We call you the Hospitable One.
From you, real forgiveness.
Father of those in need.
If you are gone, there is darkness.
Here and above in heaven.
For years without end.

("Great God," Swahili song, trans. Fr. Don Larmore)

Self-Reflection and Sharing

Use handout 3–A, "Children of God," for self-reflection and sharing. This part of the prayer can be done with small groups, large groups, or journaling groups. Details for using the handout with each of these types of groups are included in this manual's introduction, on pages 8–10.

Closing Reflection

If a meal is to follow the self-reflection and sharing, you could announce ahead of time that the meal will begin right after the self-reflection and sharing and thus the group will not have a formal gathered closing.

If you are going to have a closing reflection, the prayer in this section is offered as an option. You can either read it yourself or ask a volunteer who is a good reader to do so.

You could instead end the self-reflection and sharing with words of your own, or ask the small groups or prayer partners to end their time together with spontaneous prayer. Use whatever seems most fitting for your group, your setting, and your time schedule.

The closing prayer on the next page is actually the complete text of a child's prayer book called *Precious Moments Prayers for Boys and Girls,* by Dawn Turn. If you can get a copy of the book, reading from it would be a wonderful way to end the prayer because each page contains only one sentence and an illustration, which you can show the group. The group members will really remember what is was like having a book read to them when they were small children. Like many children's books, *Precious Moments Prayers* contains some simple basic truths that still speak to us long after we've outgrown childhood.

God, please help me start my day
    with loving thoughts and helpful ways.
As I take my bath I pray
    that you'll be with me through the day.
Thank you for this world you've given
    to care for and to live in.
I thank you, God, for all the trees
    and butterflies and birds and bees.
God, please watch me through the day
    when I work and when I play.
Lord, please bless my friends with love
    and give us guidance from above.
Before we eat, we bow our heads
    and thank you for our daily bread.
I like to read before I sleep.
    Thank you for this special treat.
Lord, please protect me and
    keep me warm and safe while I sleep.

Long Prayer

Themes

◆ the innocence and playfulness of children
◆ the Scriptures as the foundation of our faith and prayer

Background Information

This long prayer focuses on the playfulness of children and involves the building of a paper chain with favorite Bible verses.

Preparation

Supplies

❑ a paper chain
❑ a large candle, cross, or other object(s) symbolic of Christian worship
❑ *optional:* a cassette or CD player and a cassette or CD of *Still on the Journey* (Sweet Honey in the Rock, Earthbeat! Records, 1993)
❑ a large Bible on a stand
❑ one worktable if you are using method 1, two worktables if you are using method 2
❑ a strip of brightly colored construction paper for each participant (four strips 12 inches long can be cut from a 9-by-12-inch piece of construction paper)

❑ a stapler and staples
❑ a pen or marker for each participant
❑ if using method 2, Bible verses copied from handout 3–B, "Paper Chain Scriptures," and cut apart
❑ if using method 2, a basket to collect the slips of paper that contain the Scripture passages the participants chose

Setting   The room should comfortably accommodate the number of people gathered. Although many arrangements are possible, the group might do best sitting in chairs in a circle, with one or two small worktables in their midst. The amounts of space and time needed depend on how you orchestrate the building of the chain of Scripture passages. Building the chain involves making links out of strips of colored construction paper with Bible verses written on them. You may choose one of two methods for doing this:

Method 1. Write each Scripture passage given on handout 3–B, "Paper Chain Scriptures," on a strip of colored construction paper. Lay the strips out on a worktable. Invite each participant to select one passage and write her or his name on the back of the strip.

Method 2. Photocopy handout 3–B, "Paper Chain Scriptures," and cut it apart so that each Scripture passage is on its own slip of paper. Lay the slips out on one worktable. On another worktable, arrange blank, precut strips of colored construction paper and pens or markers. Have each participant choose a Scripture passage and then copy it on one of the strips of construction paper. The slips of paper from which the participants copied the Scripture passage can be collected in a basket so that you have easy access to the list of passages the group chose.

The method you use depends largely on how much time you want to spend. With either method, you should join the group in selecting and preparing a passage for the Scripture chain. Because the ending blessing mentions food and drink, it is a really good idea to plan this prayer right before a meal or snack.

Set up one central focusing area in the middle of a table or the middle of the room. Place a large Bible on a stand. Add a paper chain and a large candle, cross, or other object(s) symbolic of Christian worship.

Expectations   This prayer works equally well with junior high and senior high youth. You will notice some variations within either age-group. Some young people will spend a long time choosing their Scripture passage; others will just grab one without looking at the others. Some will want to decorate their slip of paper, and some will hardly want to sign their name.

Groups of more than fifteen participants will do better with method 1, especially groups of junior high youth. Groups of fewer than fifteen participants will do well with method 2, especially if they are high school age and older.

Procedure

Call to Prayer Say something like the following to call everyone together in the spirit of prayer:

> I welcome you in the name of our Savior, Jesus, who cautions us to become like children if we wish to be part of the kindom of God. I have used the word *kindom* instead of *kingdom*. Kingdom implies a place ruled by power, with subjects and royalty, with haves and have-nots. Kindom evokes imagery of people who care about one another because they are family or close enough to feel like family.
>
> I encourage you to get in touch with that childhood place inside of you. May we pray together today with the innocence, playfulness, trust, and humility of children.

At this point, either play the song "No Mirrors in My Nana's House," by Ysaye Maria Barnwell, or have someone with an excellent reading voice read the lyrics (below). If the lyrics will be read, first explain to the participants that they will be hearing from a person looking back on her childhood in her grandmother's house with a child's eye and seeing as good some things that a person looking with an adult's eye might not always see as good.

> There were no mirrors in my Nana's house
> No mirrors in my Nana's house
>
> And the beauty that I saw in everything,
> The beauty in everything Was in her eyes.
>
> So I never knew that my skin was too Black
> I never knew that my nose was too flat
> I never knew that my clothes didn't fit
> And I never knew there were things that I missed
> And the beauty in everything
> Was in her eyes.
>
> I was intrigued by the cracks in the walls
> The dust in the sun looked like snow that would fall
> The noise in the hallway was music to me
> The trash and the rubbish would cushion my feet
> And the beauty in everything was in her eyes.
>
> There were no mirrors in my Nana's house
> No mirrors in my Nana's house.
>
> (Sweet Honey in the Rock, *Still on the Journey*)

Scripture Reading Have an excellent reader go to the Bible, pick it up reverently, and read the following Scripture passage. If you want this touching translation, use the Good News Bible in Today's English Version or, if that version is not available, copy this translation of the passage on a card and put the card in another Bible for the reader to use.

> Young people, enjoy your youth. Be happy while you are still young. Do what you want to do, and follow your heart's desire. But remember that God is going to judge you for whatever you do.
>
> Don't let anything worry you or cause you pain. You aren't going to be young very long. (Eccles. 11:9–10, TEV)

Response Tell the group that as a response to the encouraging advice to enjoy youth and be happy, they will make paper chains out of Bible verses.

If you are using method 1, have the participants go to the worktable and look through the Bible verses written on the strips of construction paper. When they find one they like, direct them to write their name on the opposite side of the strip of paper and then to sit back down with it and wait for the others to finish.

If you are using method 2, have the participants go to the first worktable, where they will find all the slips of paper with the Bible verses printed on them. Ask them to choose a passage they like and then go to the second worktable and write their passage on one of the blank strips of construction paper. They also need to put their name on the back of the strip. When they are finished, have them put in the basket the printed slip of paper from which they copied their Scripture passage. Tell them to keep the construction paper strip on which they copied their verse, and to sit down and wait until the others are finished.

When everyone is finished, and the printed slips, pens, and extra construction paper strips are cleaned up, the group can begin putting together their paper chain of Scriptures.

Explain to the group that you would like each person to read aloud the Scripture passage he or she chose, and then staple his or her strip into the paper chain.

You should start the process. Read your Scripture passage, tell what book of the Bible it comes from, and then bend your strip into a circle and staple the ends together. (If you are with mature participants who seemed to take time choosing their Scripture passage, you might say something about why you chose that particular verse, and ask the others to do the same when it is their turn.)

Then hand your paper link to the next person, along with the stapler. That person will read her or his Scripture passage (explain her or his reasons for choosing it, if you have asked for some comments), bend the strip of paper so that it forms a circle that goes through the first circle, and staple the strip together in that position. The result should be two connected paper links, the beginning of a chain.

Each person continues until the chain is finished.

When the stapler and chain return to you, hang up the chain in the room and keep it there as a decoration and a reminder of the Scriptures.

Final Blessing   Send the group forth with these words:

> It's time for us to extend our celebration of childhood into our mealtime. We go forth to our food and drink with these words of encouragement from the Scriptures: "Go ahead—eat your food and be happy; drink your wine and be cheerful. It's all right with God" (Eccles. 9:7, TEV).

Family Component

Details for using the family component are included on pages 11–12 of the introduction to this book. Here are a list of the supplies you will need and a reminder of the settings in which the family component can be used.

Supplies   ❑ handout 3–C, "Families of Children of God"
❑ sample 3–A, "Sample Letter for Families"

Settings   ◆ a gathering of families after a retreat or long event
◆ a separate gathering of youth and families
◆ a bulletin or parish newsletter insert
◆ a personal letter and take-home handout
◆ a follow-up mailing

Children of God

Scripture Reading

Train children in the right way,
and when old, they will not
stray.
(Proverbs 22:6, NRSV)

Questions

✦ What's the right way to train or
teach children?
✦ Have you been trained in that way?
How do you know?
✦ What's the right way to train or
teach teenagers?
✦ Have you been trained in that way?
How do you know?
✦ What's the right way to train or teach adults?
✦ Do you train the adults you know in that way? Why or why not?

Scripture Reading

Do not let anyone look down on you because you are young, but be
an example for the believers in your speech, your conduct, your love,
faith, and purity. (1 Timothy 4:12, TEV)

Questions

✦ Has someone ever looked down on you because of your youth? If so,
what happened? How did it feel?
✦ When have you been a positive example to others through your
speech, conduct, love, faith, or purity (or any other way)?
✦ Are you more often an example for children who are younger than you
are, or for adults who are older than you are? Why?

Scripture Reading

All who are led by the Spirit of God are children of God. (Romans
8:14, NRSV)

Questions

✦ What does it mean to be "led by the Spirit of God"? Has the Spirit ever
led you? If so, to where or what were you led? What happened?
✦ Do you like being called a child of God? Does that name make you feel
as if your status is being raised or lowered? Why?
✦ What is the status of a child in today's world? of a teenager? of an
adult? of an elderly person?
✦ Why would age change a person's status? Are age-related status
changes beneficial in any way? Where do these status changes come
from?
✦ What is the status of God in today's world?

Handout 3-A: Permission to reproduce this handout for use in your program is granted.

55

Paper Chain Scriptures

When the rainbow appears in the clouds, I will see it and remember the everlasting covenant between me and all living things on earth.

(Genesis 9:16, TEV)

"Blessed are those who are poor in spirit:
the kindom of heaven is theirs."
(Matthew 5:3, INT)

I give thanks to my God each time I remember you, and when I pray for you, I pray with joy. I cannot forget all you shared with me in the service of the Gospel, from the first day until now.

(Philippians 1:3–5, CCB)

Clap your hands for joy, all peoples!
Praise God with loud songs!
(Psalm 47:1, TEV)

We know that God makes everything work together for the good of those who love God and have been called according to God's purpose.

(Romans 8:28, INT)

May the LORD bless you and take care of you;
May the LORD be kind and gracious to you;
May the LORD look on you
with favor and give you peace.
(Numbers 6:24–27, TEV)

Yes, God so loved the world
as to give the Only Begotten One,
that whoever believes may not die,
but have eternal life.
(John 3:16, INT)

You will never go hungry or ever be in need. . . . You will have all you want to eat, and you will give thanks to the Lord your God.

(Deuteronomy 8:9–10, TEV)

Meanwhile these three remain: faith, hope, and love; and the greatest of these is love.

(1 Corinthians 13:13, TEV)

"Be strong and stand firm. Be fearless and undaunted, for go where you may, Yahweh your God is with you."

(Joshua 1:9, NJB)

"Where your treasure is, there your heart will be also."
(Matthew 6:21, NRSV)

Rejoice in the Lord always. I say it again: rejoice and may everyone experience your gentle and understanding heart. The Lord is near; do not be anxious about anything.

(Philippians 4:4–6, CCB)

"'Speak, Lord, your servant is listening.'"
(1 Samuel 3:9, TEV)

We give thanks to God at all times for you and remember you in our prayers.

(1 Thessalonians 1:3, CCB)

"I am the way, and the truth, and the life."
(John 14:6, NRSV)

Pray at all times as the Spirit inspires you.
(Ephesians 6:18, CCB)

Yahweh, my God, I take refuge in you.
(Psalm 7:1, NJB)

"Ask, and it will be given to you; seek and you will find; knock and the door will be opened to you. For everyone who asks, receives; and the one who seeks, finds; and to the one who knocks, the door will be opened."
(Matthew 7:7–8, NAB)

All who are led by the Spirit of God are children of God.
(Romans 8:14, NRSV)

"God is great!"
(Psalm 70:4, NRSV)

We ask you, brothers and sisters, to respect those who labor among you, who have charge over you in Christ as your teachers. Esteem them highly, with a special love because of their work. Live in peace with each other.
(1 Thessalonians 5:12–13, INT)

"Go, then, to all peoples everywhere and make them my disciples: baptize them."

(Matthew 28:19, TEV)

Go ahead—eat your food and be happy; drink your wine and be cheerful. It's all right with God. Always look happy and cheerful.
(Ecclesiastes 9:7–8, TEV)

Do not let anyone look down on you because you are young, but be an example for the believers in your speech, your conduct, your love, faith, and purity.

(1 Timothy 4:12, TEV)

"I came so that they might have life and have it more abundantly."
(John 10:10, NAB)

Sing a new song to Yahweh!
Sing to Yahweh, all the earth!
(Psalm 96:1, NJB)

Dear friends, let us love one another, because love comes from God. Whoever loves is a child of God and knows God.

(1 John 4:7, TEV)

The community of believers was of one mind and one heart. None of them claimed anything as their own; rather, everything was held in common.
(Acts 4:32, INT)

How wonderful it is, how pleasant,
for God's people to live together in harmony!
(Psalm 133:1, TEV)

Walk in love as Christ loved us.
(Ephesians 5:2, INT)

"I am with you always, until the end of the age."
(Matthew 28:20, NAB)

Alleluia!
Praise Yahweh, my soul!
I will praise Yahweh all my life,
I will make music to my God as long as I live.
(Psalm 146:1, NJB)

"The truth is, whoever doesn't welcome the kindom of God as a little child won't enter it."

(Mark 10:15, INT)

Train children in the right way,
and when old, they will not stray.
(Proverbs 22:6, NRSV)

"There is nothing that God cannot do."
(Luke 1:37, TEV)

There is a season for everything, a time for every occupation under heaven.
(Ecclesiastes 3:1, NJB)

"The angels of God rejoice over one sinner who repents."
(Luke 15:10, TEV)

A loyal friend is like a safe shelter; find one, and you have found a treasure. Nothing else is as valuable; there is no way of putting a price on it. A loyal friend is like a medicine that keeps you in good health.
(Sirach 6:14–16, TEV)

God is love.
(1 John 4:8, TEV)

- ✂ - - - - - -

Make every effort to keep among you the unity of Spirit through the bonds of peace. Let there be one body and one spirit, for God, in calling you, gave the same Spirit to all. One Lord, one faith, one baptism.

(Ephesians 4:3–5, CCB)

- -

"Blessed are those who work for peace:
they will be called children of God."
(Matthew 5:9, INT)

- -

"Do not be afraid—I will save you.
I have called you by name—you are mine."
(Isaiah 43:1, TEV)

- -

"I am the good shepherd."
(John 10:11, TEV)

- -

Cast all your cares on God, who cares for you.
(1 Peter 5:7, INT)

- -

"Respect your father and your mother, so that you may live a long time in the land that I am giving you."

(Exodus 20:12, TEV)

- -

In the beginning was the Word:
the Word was with God
and the Word was God.
(John 1:1, NJB)

- -

"I shall give you a new heart, and put a new spirit in you; I shall remove the heart of stone from your bodies and give you a heart of flesh instead."
(Ezekiel 36:26, NJB)

- -

Do not worry about tomorrow; it will have enough worries of its own.
(Matthew 6:34, TEV)

- -

Let justice flow like a stream, and righteousness like a river that never goes dry.

(Amos 5:24, TEV)

- -

"Only believe."
(Mark 5:36, NRSV)

"You have already been told what is right
and what Yahweh wants of you.
Only this, to do what is right,
to love loyalty
and to walk humbly with your God."
(Micah 6:8, NJB)

"My grace is all you need, for my power is greatest when you are weak."
(2 Corinthians 12:9, TEV)

Give me the Wisdom that sits beside your throne; give me a place among
your children.
(Wisdom of Solomon 9:4, TEV)

"I am the vine, you are the branches."
(John 15:5, NRSV)

"As for my family and me, we will serve the LORD."
(Joshua 24:15, TEV)

May Christ dwell in your hearts through faith.
May you be rooted and founded in love.
(Ephesians 3:17, CCB)

Be sincere and determined. Keep calm when trouble comes. Stay with the
Lord.
(Sirach 2:2–3, TEV)

"You are the salt of the earth. . . . You are the light of the world."
(Matthew 5:13–14, NRSV)

Young people, enjoy your youth. Be happy while you are still young. Do
what you want to do, and follow your heart's desire.
(Ecclesiastes 11:9, TEV)

"I am the resurrection and the life."
(John 11:25, NRSV)

✂

"God is with you in everything you do."
(Genesis 21:22, TEV)

Now then, give praise to the God of the universe, who has done great things everywhere, who brings us up from the time we are born, and deals with us mercifully.

(Sirach 50:22, TEV)

You are always in my heart! And so it is only right for me to feel as I do about you.

(Philippians 1:7, TEV)

Yahweh is my light and my salvation,
whom should I fear?
(Psalm 27:1, NJB)

"Come to me, all you that are weary and are carrying heavy burdens, and I will give you rest. Take my yoke upon you, and learn from me; for I am gentle and humble in heart, and you will find rest for your souls. For my yoke is easy, and my burden is light."

(Matthew 11:28–30, NRSV)

Families of Children of God

As a family, you could sit down and go over this meditation together. One family member might read the first Scripture reading, and another family member, the set of questions that follows. Then you could share your answers to the questions, along with any other insights you may have.

You might want to select a toy from your home to keep on or near your kitchen table to remind your family that all of you are children of God.

Scripture Reading

Train children in the right way,
and when old, they will not stray.

(Proverbs 22:6, NRSV)

Questions
✦ Think of a time when an older family member (or friend) taught you something important that you have never forgotten. How were you taught?
✦ Think of a time when you helped an older family member (or friend) learn something. What happened?

Scripture Reading

Do not let anyone look down on you because you are young, but be an example for the believers in your speech, your conduct, your love, faith, and purity. (1 Timothy 4:12, TEV)

Questions
✦ Has someone ever looked down on you because you were young?
✦ Do you think that you are more often an example for children who are younger than you are, for adults who are older than you, or for people your own age? Why?
✦ Who in your family do you look up to? Why?

Scripture Reading

All who are led by the Spirit of God are children of God. (Romans 8:14, NRSV)

Questions
✦ What do you think it means to be a child of God? Can a very old man or woman still be a child of God? If so, how?
✦ Can you recall a time when you almost did something wrong but somehow the Spirit of God led you to do the right thing instead? If so, what happened?

Handout 3-C: Permission to reproduce this handout for use in your program is granted.

63

Sample Letter for Families

Dear _____,

It has been a pleasure having _____ with us. Thank you for making all the necessary family arrangements so that <u>she/he</u> could be with us. It was truly a gift from your family to our parish community.

During our time together, we focused on being children of God. In fact, we shared a prayer experience based on children. You might ask _____ what <u>he/she</u> thought of the experience.

Enclosed is a family-based version of a reflection prayer we used. I encourage you to take some time during or after a family meal to go through the questions and discuss them as a family. You could even spend some time talking about different stories from your childhood. Keeping a family toy on the kitchen counter or table for a while might also serve as a reminder of your family commitment to be faithful children of God. These are just a few ideas to help you get in touch with _____'s experience with this prayer.

If you have any questions about our programs, or if any of your family members would like to become more involved with our parish in any way, please don't hesitate to call me. I wish your family great peace and joy.

Sincerely,

_____

Index of Scriptural Passages

This index lists the Scripture passages cited in all four books of *Prayer Works*. Each Scripture passage is followed by a book number, a colon, and a page number or numbers.

Sample entry:

Genesis

2:4–7   2:52

The sample entry tells you that a reference to Genesis 2:4–7 can be found on page 52 of book 2 of *Prayer Works*.

scriptural passage	book, page
Genesis	
2:4–7	2:52
6:9—9:17	3:37–38
9:16	1:56
21:22	1:62
43:11	2:41, 2:42
Exodus	
2:23—3:12	2:52–53
3:17	4:15
20:12	1:60
Numbers	
6:24–27	1:56
7:13	4:16
Deuteronomy	
8:9–10	1:56
Joshua	
1:9	1:57
24:15	1:61
1 Samuel	
3:9	1:57
2 Samuel	
22:47	1:15, 1:22, 1:23, 1:26

scriptural passage	book, page
Psalms	
7:1	1:57
8	4:60
9:1–2	4:60
16:3,5–6,9–11	4:60
18:1–2,49	1:21
18:1–3	4:60
18:31,46	2:57, 2:58
18:46	1:15, 1:22, 2:49
19:1–6	4:61
23	4:61
27:1	1:62
27:1–5	4:61
29	4:61
33:1–5	4:62
37:3–6	4:62
45	4:62
47	4:62
47:1	1:56
65:1–5,9–13	3:18, 3:24
65:9–13	4:62
70:4	1:58
81:16	4:15
91	4:63
96	4:63
96:1	1:58
100	4:63
103	4:63
104:1,24,31,33–35	4:56
107:1,23–30	4:64
112:1–5	4:64
118:24–29	2:15
121	4:64
122	4:64
127	4:65
131	4:65
133	4:65
133:1	1:58
134	4:65
136	4:65
139	4:66
146:1	1:59
147:1,4,8,14	4:66
147:12–18	4:50
150	4:66

scriptural passage	book, page
Proverbs	
22:6	1:55, 1:59, 1:63
Ecclesiastes	
3:1	1:59, 3:37
9:7	1:54
9:7–8	1:58
11:9	1:61
11:9–10	1:53
Isaiah	
43:1	1:60
43:1–7	2:21
49:15–16	2:21
Ezekiel	
36:26	1:60
47:12	1:40, 1:42
Amos	
5:24	1:60
Jonah	
1:1—4:11	3:38–39
Micah	
6:8	1:61
Judith	
15:12–13	2:25, 2:26
Wisdom of Solomon	
9:4	1:61
Sirach	
2:2–3	1:61
6:14–16	1:59
43:11–20	3:41
50:22	1:62

scriptural passage	book, page
Matthew	
5:3	1:56
5:9	1:60
5:13	4:15
5:13–14	1:61
5:39	2:31
6:19–21	2:37
6:21	1:57
6:22	3:53, 3:66
6:34	1:60
7:7–8	1:57
7:24–27	2:53
11:28–30	1:62
13:8	4:27, 4:28, 4:29
13:30	4:27, 4:28, 4:29
16:25	2:31
18:3–4	1:47
20:16	2:31
22:37–40	3:56
28:19	1:58
28:20	1:59
Mark	
1:6–11	3:15
3:21	2:31
4:35–41	3:40
5:36	1:61
10:15	1:59
Luke	
1:37	1:59
6:46–49	2:53
15:10	1:59
18:9–14	4:38

scriptural passage	book, page
John	
1:1	1:60
3:8	2:49, 2:57, 2:59
3:16	1:56
4:5–42	2:54–55
6:48–51	4:22
8:12	2:49, 2:57, 2:58
10:10	1:58
10:11	1:60
11:25	1:61
12:24	4:27, 4:28, 4:29
13:3–17	3:21
14:6	1:57
15:5	1:61
15:5–6	1:31
Acts of the Apostles	
4:32	1:58
Romans	
8:14	1:55, 1:57, 1:63
8:28	1:56
1 Corinthians	
1:27–30	1:36
5:6	4:16
13:13	1:25, 1:57
2 Corinthians	
4:6–7	1:36
6:6–7	1:25
9:10	4:27
11:18–21	2:31
11:23–33	4:35
12:7	4:34
12:9	1:61, 2:31, 4:34
13:11–13	4:58, 4:67

scriptural passage	book, page
Galatians	
5:22–23	1:25
Ephesians	
1:15–18	3:51
3:17	1:61
4:3–5	1:60
5:2	1:59
6:18	1:57
Philippians	
1:3–5	1:56
1:7	1:62
4:4–6	1:57
Colossians	
3:12–13	1:25
1 Thessalonians	
1:3	1:57
5:12–13	1:58
1 Timothy	
4:12	1:55, 1:58, 1:63
1 Peter	
5:7	1:60
1 John	
4:7	1:58
4:8	1:59
Revelation	
22:1,17	2:57, 2:59
22:17	2:49

Index of Themes

This index lists the topical and cultural themes cited in all four books of *Prayer Works*. Each theme is followed by a book number, a colon, and a page number or numbers.

Sample entry:
baptism, 3:14–16

The sample entry tells you that a prayer with a baptismal theme can be found on pages 14–16 of book 3 of *Prayer Works*.

Acknowledgments *(continued)*

The scriptural quotations identified as NRSV are from the New Revised Standard Version of the Bible. Copyright © 1989 by the Division of Christian Education of the National Council of the Churches of Christ in the United States of America. All rights reserved.

The scriptural quotations identified as NAB are from the New American Bible with revised Psalms and revised New Testament. Copyright © 1986, 1991 by the Confraternity of Christian Doctrine, 3211 Fourth Street NE, Washington, DC 20017. Used with permission. All rights reserved.

The scriptural quotations identified as TEV are from Today's English Version. Second edition copyright © 1966, 1971, 1976, 1992 by the American Bible Society. Used by permission. All rights reserved.

The scriptural quotations identified as CCB are from the Christian Community Bible, second edition. Copyright © 1988 by Bernardo Hurault. Used by permission. All rights reserved.

The scriptural quotations identified as NJB are from the New Jerusalem Bible. Copyright © 1985 by Darton, Longman and Todd, London, and Doubleday, a division of Bantam Doubleday Dell Publishing Group, New York. Reprinted by permission.

The scriptural quotations identified as INT are from the Inclusive New Testament by Priests for Equality. Copyright © 1994 by Priests for Equality. Used with permission. All rights reserved.

All other scriptural quotations in this book are freely adapted and are not to be interpreted or used as official translations of the Scriptures.

The excerpts on pages 15 and 25 are from *Sacred Ground: Reflections on Lakota Spirituality and the Gospel,* by Ron Zeilinger, M Div. (Chamberlain, SD: Tipi Press, 1986), pages 68–70 and 56, 60, 61–62. Used with permission.

The poem "The Rock," by Lloyd Carl Owl, on pages 17, 24, and 27 is from *American Indian Prayers and Poetry,* edited by J. Ed Sharpe (Marietta, GA: Cherokee Publications, 1985), no page. Copyright © 1985 by Cherokee Publications. Permission applied for.

The excerpt on page 31 by Swami Prabhupada is from *Srimad Bhagavatam,* canto 1, page 62. Copyright © 1972, 1976, 1978 by Bhaktivedanta Book Trust. All rights reserved.

The prayer "The Cathedral of the Serengeti," on page 33, was written by Fr. Don Larmore, a missionary to Africa.

The Swahili song "Great God," quoted on page 49, was translated by Fr. Don Larmore.

The prayer on page 50 is from *Precious Moments Prayers for Boys and Girls,* by Dawn Turn (Farmingdale, NY: Regina Press, 1994). Copyright © 1994 by Precious Moments. Permission applied for.

The lyrics on page 52 from "No Mirrors in My Nana's House," by Ysaye Maria Barnwell, are from the album *Still on the Journey,* by Sweet Honey in the Rock, 9 42536-4. Copyright © 1993 EarthBeat! Records, Redway, California. Permission applied for.